1990
4/90

Otters, Octopuses, and Odd Creatures of the Deep

Otters, Octopuses, and Odd Creatures of the Deep

Randall A. Reinstedt

Illustrated by David F. Aguero

Ghost Town Publications
Carmel, California

The History and Happenings of California Series
Published by
Ghost Town Publications
P.O. Drawer 5998
Carmel, California 93921

Manufactured in the United States of America

Library of Congress Catalog Number 87-82106
ISBN 0-933818-21-1

Edited by John Bergez
Book design and art direction by Sharon Kinghan-Berkheimer

*This book is dedicated to the many
Monterey fishermen who shared with me
their knowledge and tales of days gone by*

MOSS LANDING

SANTA CRUZ

MONTEREY BAY

MONTEREY SUBMARINE CANYON

MONTEREY PENINSULA

SAN FRANCISCO

MONTEREY BAY

CALIFORNIA

PACIFIC OCEAN

LOS ANGELES

N

Sometimes adventure is all around you, if you only know where to look.

That's what Johnny Nelson's dad was always saying, but one rainy Saturday in Monterey, Johnny didn't know where to look. And that was driving Jody Cooper crazy. "Keep Johnny company while his mother and I are visiting," her mom had said. But Johnny was two years younger than Jody, and so far he hadn't liked any of her ideas for ways to spend the afternoon.

"Maybe we can play a game," Jody suggested as she and Johnny rummaged around in her bedroom closet. She pulled out a deck of cards. "How about—"

"*Cards?*" Johnny exclaimed, rolling his eyes. "You mean like 'Go Fish'? Bor-*ing!*"

"Well, what *can* we do?" Jody answered with a scowl. "It's still raining outside, and your mom says you can't get wet. So playing with your skateboard is out."

"It's not my fault that it's raining," Johnny pouted. "I wish I could have stayed home in Sacramento." Glumly he sat down on the bed and stared out the window at the light rain drifting down on the garden. "Does it always rain in Monterey?"

Jody sighed as she put her deck of cards away. "You know, Johnny, I didn't ask you to visit. If you weren't here I'd probably be doing my homework, and I know you'd think that sixth-grade homework was super boring!"

"I didn't ask to come either! I can't help it if our moms like to sit and talk for hours and hours. You know something, Jody? Grownups are bor-*ing.*"

"I guess they are," Jody agreed. Suddenly she snapped her fingers. "I know what we can do. Come on, get your coat. We'll go next door and see Vito."

"Who's Vito?"

"A grownup who's not boring," Jody replied, pulling on a raincoat. "Come on! Let's go ask our moms if it's okay."

7

"But who is he?"

"You'll see!" said Jody, and she hurried off to the kitchen to find their mothers. With a shrug, Johnny fetched his coat and followed her.

"I suppose it would be all right," Mrs. Cooper was saying as Johnny came in. She glanced over her coffee cup at Johnny's mother. "Vito," she explained, "is a retired fisherman who lives next door. He's full of old fishing stories, but he's very good with young people. Who knows, maybe he can figure out a way to entertain these two characters." Turning to Jody, she said, "Just be sure Vito isn't busy, dear."

"And don't get too wet," added Johnny's mother.

"Aw, I don't want to talk to an old fisherman," complained Johnny. "Who wants to hear a bunch of fish stories?"

"I know," Jody sighed. "That's bor-*ing!*"

"Oh, go on," urged Johnny's mother as she poured herself more coffee. "Maybe this Vito fellow can help you two get along better."

"It's either that or homework," said Jody.

"Oh, all right," Johnny muttered, buttoning his coat. "But this is sure turning out to be one boring Saturday."

Vito

Dodging puddles, Jody and Johnny hurried through the rain to Vito's house. On the porch, a weathered brass ship's bell hung from a rusty chain.

"Hold your ears!" Jody warned as she swung the bell's clapper. An ear-splitting clang rang through the neighborhood.

"Some doorbell!" Johnny shouted over the noise. "Is the old guy deaf or something?"

"Not just yet, son," said a voice from behind them. Startled, Johnny turned around to see a tall, bearded man in a heavy blue coat and a faded fisherman's cap standing at the foot of the porch.

"Vito!" Jody exclaimed, shooting Johnny a dirty look. Johnny blushed.

"Didn't mean to sneak up on you," Vito said with a smile. "But I was just on my way to the garage when I heard that old bell a-clankin'. So what brings you two landlubbers out on a day such as this?"

"I guess we're bored," Jody answered.

9

"Is that so?" Vito replied. He looked curiously at Johnny.

Jody nodded. "Well, one of us is. Oh, I almost forgot, this is Johnny Nelson. He's from Sacramento and he's in the fourth grade. My mom and his mom went to school together. While they're busy talking, we're supposed to be entertaining each other."

"I see." Vito climbed the steps to the porch. "Well, it's very nice to meet you, young man," he said. His dark eyes seemed to be studying Johnny carefully, as if Johnny were a strange new creature Vito had found in his fishing net. "Very nice indeed." He held out his hand.

As Johnny shook hands, he winced from the strength of Vito's grip. Jody's fisherman friend wasn't anything like the bent old man he had imagined. Vito stood straight and tall. His long hair and bushy beard were snow white, but his cheeks were leathery brown. Along one side of his nose there was a thin, pale line—a scar, Johnny thought to himself.

"Yeah," he found himself saying as he took a step backwards, trying not to rub the hand that Vito had just released. "I thought I could play with my skateboard, but with the rain and all . . . We just can't think of anything we both like to do."

"That's a predicament," Vito agreed. He rubbed his nose thoughtfully. "Hm, what to do on a rainy day?"

"Something besides cards," Johnny pleaded.

"Well, as it happens I was just getting the truck out to drive down to the Monterey Bay Aquarium," Vito said. "You're welcome to tag along if you want."

"That would be super!" Jody exclaimed. "I've only been there a couple of times, and I've never seen it all. Maybe we'll get to see my old fourth-grade teacher, Mr. Larson. He works there on weekends sometimes."

Johnny wrinkled his nose. "Aw, I don't want to go see a bunch of boring fish. We've got all the fish we need in the Sacramento River behind my house."

"There's a lot more than fish in that aquarium, Johnny," Vito corrected him. "As a matter of fact, there's a couple of creatures that make your Sacramento River fish seem pretty tame."

"Like what?" Johnny asked.

"Oh, for one thing, a beast that shoots around the water like it had its own jet engine," Vito replied. "Why, when this critter loses an arm, it doesn't even fret! All it has to do is grow another one." Vito laid a hand on Johnny's shoulder. "Take it from an old fisherman, son. There are more strange and wonderful things in those waters out there than you can imagine."

"Okay, okay, I'm convinced," Johnny said half-heartedly. "Let's go see the aquarium."

"That-a-boy! I'm sure you won't be disappointed." Vito gave Johnny a friendly pat. "Jody, tell your mother we'll go in my pickup, so you won't get too wet. And ask her if she can pick you up, because I'll be staying down on the Row 'til after dark."

"Okay, Vito!" Jody replied gaily. "Johnny, you wait here." Putting her mouth to his ear, she whispered, "And be nice."

Cannery Row

As Jody ran home, Johnny asked Vito what the "Row" was.

"Oh, that's short for Cannery Row, Johnny. That's the street the aquarium is on. It got its name from a book called *Cannery Row*. Ever heard of it?"

Johnny shook his head.

"It was written by a famous writer who used to live around here. His name was John Steinbeck. Back in the days when Steinbeck was working on his book, that street was lined with canneries—places where they canned sardines. In those days Monterey was called the Sardine Capital of the World!"

Johnny was unimpressed. "That's a funny thing to be famous for," he said.

"Maybe so, but the fact is that people figured more sardines were caught around here than in any other place in the world. Why, there were a hundred boats or more, going out there in the bay and hauling in thousands of those silvery little critters on every trip. My crews and I brought in quite a few tons ourselves, before the fish just up and disappeared on us. Those were dark days, when the sardines stopped coming."

"What happened to them?"

Before Vito could reply, Jody came running up the steps to the porch.

"We're all set," she said breathlessly. "My mom will pick us up at the entrance about four o'clock."

"We'd best be on our way then," said Vito. "All aboard, mates, the truck's around back."

Vito's truck was a battered old pickup with fishing nets piled high in the back. As he climbed into the cab, Johnny sniffed and grabbed his nose. "Wow, you must have been carrying fish in here," he gasped.

"Ah, yes, doesn't it smell grand?" chuckled Vito. "I didn't haul fish in here, but the smell does cling to things. To me that's the sweet smell of success."

"Success phooey! It's the smell of rotten fish!" exclaimed Johnny through his pinched nose.

"Now, now, let's not argue," giggled Jody. But as she slammed the door shut, her eyes grew wide. "What a nice smell, Vito," she gulped politely. She wondered whether she could hold her breath all the way to the aquarium.

With a grin, Vito started the engine and they were off. As they rumbled and creaked down the hill toward Cannery Row, Vito told Johnny and Jody about how the aquarium had been built on the site of an old cannery. "But the history of that location goes back a lot farther than that," he added. "Back about the turn of the century, before the cannery was built, that area was right by Chinatown."

"I didn't know we had a Chinatown here," said Jody. "I know there's one in San Francisco."

"And in Los Angeles, too," Vito pointed out. "But Monterey's was different. It was a Chinese fishing village. Quite a colorful place it was, too. There were houses built on stilts over the water, and lots of Oriental-style fishing boats. People said it reminded them of fishing villages they'd seen in China."

"Is it all gone?" asked Jody. "I've never seen any houses like that."

Vito nodded grimly. "A mysterious fire burned the village down many years ago. There were those who said that people couldn't stand the stink of the squid and fish when they were laid out to dry. Can you imagine that?"

"Er, no," Jody replied in a strangled voice.

"That fire was a terrible thing," Vito continued. "Later on, the canneries went up, and the warehouses. Look, we're coming to the Row now. Those older buildings you see are all that's left of Cannery Row." The old man shook his head sadly. "Of course, it's mostly restaurants and shops and hotels now. In my day, canneries and warehouses stretched along both sides of this street for almost a mile. Millions of dollars' worth of fish were brought in during the sardine season. I read somewhere that if you could lay one season's catch of sardines from end to end, they'd stretch almost from the earth to the moon! There were so many people working on the Row, you could hardly drive through here either day or night." Vito chuckled. "You think my truck smells bad, Johnny? Back when the sardine was king, this whole end of town had the sweet smell of success!"

"Pew! I'm glad I wasn't here then," Jody laughed.

"But what happened?" Johnny asked impatiently. "Where did all of the fish go?"

Vito shrugged. "That's something of a puzzle, Johnny. You'd probably get a different answer from each person you asked. All anyone knows for sure is that around the mid-1940s they started to disappear. It wasn't too many years before there wasn't a single sardine left to catch."

"Maybe the fish finally got smart and moved somewhere else," guessed Johnny.

14

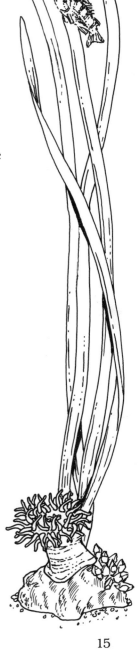

"Or maybe the currents changed and took them away," Jody suggested.

"Those are good guesses," Vito replied. "Some people say pollution was the culprit. Other people think that sardines go through a cycle and that we just have to wait for them to come back. Me, I'm guessing that we just plain fished them out. All those tons we brought in, all those years!" The old fisherman sighed. "Maybe we needed to learn not to be so greedy and to conserve what we have, instead of taking all we could get. There are those who say the sardine is starting to make a comeback, but it won't matter to us old-timers. Our day is gone, just like the canneries down here on the Row. But that's enough about the old days. Here's one cannery that has some real live fish in it!" Vito pointed to a big gray building on the edge of the water.

"Look, Johnny, the aquarium!" Jody cried. Johnny sighed. He was starting to enjoy the truck ride, but he was sure the aquarium would be bor-*ing.*

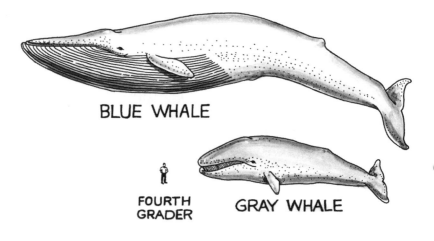

BLUE WHALE

FOURTH
GRADER   GRAY WHALE

The Biggest Animal in the World

"Okay, mates, here we are," Vito announced as he
brought the truck to a rattling halt in the aquarium's
parking lot. "Last one inside is a wet fish!" Together they
hurried to the entrance, and in a few minutes Vito was
leading them down the aquarium's Marine Mammal Hall.

"Quite a place, eh, Johnny?" Vito asked, wiping rain
water from his face and beard.

"I guess so," Johnny replied absent-mindedly. Suddenly
he stopped to stare at a huge whale that was suspended
from the ceiling. "Hey, is that real?" he asked.

"Looks like she's swimming through the air, doesn't she?
That impressive creature is made out of fiberglass, Johnny.
She's a lifesize model of a female gray whale. She's a good
deal longer than a lot of fishing boats."

Jody whistled softly. "Just think, Johnny," she said
excitedly, "whales like that come right into Monterey Bay.
There might be some out there right now."

"There probably are," Vito agreed, "along with some other
creatures you'd rather not meet!"

16

"You mean sharks?" Jody asked.

"Sharks—and other things," Vito muttered.

"I'm just wondering," Johnny said thoughtfully, "if that's a female, how big do the males get?"

"Well, now, I'm not sure," Vito replied. "Here comes one of the guides, though. Maybe he knows."

"Hey, that's Mr. Larson!" exclaimed Jody. She waved her hand. "Oh, Mr. Larson! Can we ask you a question?"

As Mr. Larson approached, his face broke into a wide smile. "Well, hello, little lady," he said, peering over his glasses. "I thought I recognized you. What brings you here this fine day?"

Jody laughed. "The rain, I guess. Johnny and I were stuck for something to do, and Vito brought us down to the aquarium."

"Vito Bruno! Well, I'll be darned," said Mr. Larson as he and Vito shook hands. "Telling these young folk your tall tales, eh, Captain?"

Johnny and Jody exchanged glances. "Captain?" whispered Johnny. Jody shrugged and shook her head. "He's just plain old Vito to me," she whispered back.

"Now, now, Bill, I only tell true tales," Vito was saying. "I was just explaining to Johnny here about the whales we sometimes see in and about the bay."

"I see. And did the captain explain, Johnny, what the whales were doing?"

Johnny shook his head.

"I know!" Jody cried. "They're migrating—all the way from Alaska down to Baja California and back."

Mr. Larson nodded approvingly. "And we see them locally from about December to May or so. As Captain Bruno may have told you, whaling was quite an important industry in California at one time. Back in the 1850s ... "

"Excuse me, Mr. Larson," Jody interrupted, "but is Vito a real captain?"

Mr. Larson raised his eyebrows in surprise. "Hasn't he

told you? Captain Bruno here was the skipper of one of the finest purse seiners in Monterey Bay. That's a fishing boat, you know. As a matter of fact, we go back a long way together. My father was one of the crew on Captain Bruno's boat."

"Those days are long gone, Bill," smiled the old fisherman. "I'm just Vito now. But I think we're forgetting something. Didn't you have a question for Mr. Larson, Johnny?"

"Oh... yeah." Trying to imagine Vito as a Captain, Johnny had forgotten all about whales. He wondered what other secrets the old fisherman might have, especially where he had gotten that scar. But he knew it would not be polite to ask.

"Yeah, um, Vito said that big whale up there was a female. I wanted to know how big the males get."

"That's a good question, Johnny," Mr. Larson answered. "To the best of my knowledge, the male doesn't get much bigger than the female. That lovely specimen above your head is forty-three feet long, and the biggest gray whales are around fifty feet. Plenty big, but not the biggest of all whales by any means."

"The biggest are the great blues," Vito commented. "I've seen a number of them in my time, and believe me, they make the grays look pretty small by comparison."

"Really?" Johnny frowned as he studied the model hanging from the ceiling. "They can't be that much bigger."

"That's where you're wrong, my friend," Mr. Larson corrected him. "There have been reports of blue whales more than twice as long as the largest grays. That's more than one hundred feet."

"One hundred feet! I bet that's longer than a couple of school buses," said Jody.

"Quite a bit longer," Mr. Larson agreed.

"Ha!" Vito snorted. "You want to compare whales and school buses? Would you believe that a good-sized blue

18

whale would weigh more than a dozen school buses?"

"Wow! How many pounds is that?" asked Jody.

"Oh, they get up to around one hundred and fifty tons," answered Mr. Larson. "That's three hundred thousand pounds. If that's hard to imagine, think of it this way. Last year the average weight of my fourth-graders was about seventy-five pounds. Johnny, at that rate, how many fourth-graders would you have to pile on a scale to balance the weight of one great blue whale?"

Johnny wrinkled his nose. "That's too hard for me. A lot, I guess."

"I'll say," Mr. Larson replied. "How about four thousand fourth-graders?"

"Four thousand!" Jody exclaimed, shaking her head. "Just think—four thousand little Johnnys!" She broke into a giggle. "I think I'd take the whale any day." Johnny stuck out his tongue.

"You must remember, though," continued Mr. Larson, "we're talking about some of the biggest creatures that have ever lived—bigger than elephants, bigger than mastodons. Why, the blue whales living in the ocean today would make most of the dinosaurs feel like small fry."

"It's no wonder sailors called them monsters of the deep," remarked Vito.

Mr. Larson held up a hand. "Ah, but these are the gentlest 'monsters' you'd ever want to meet, and the smartest, too. It's a great pity that man took it in his head to hunt them. You know, Johnny, if you're lucky you might get to see one someday. Even though blue whales are usually found out in the ocean, they do sometimes visit the California coast, including Monterey Bay."

"Is that because they're looking for food?" asked Jody.

Mr. Larson nodded. "Could be. And the bay's great Submarine Canyon might have something to do with their visits, too."

"You mean the Monterey trench," Vito remarked.

"Some people call it that," Mr. Larson agreed.

"Will someone please tell me what you're talking about?" interrupted Johnny impatiently.

"We'll do better than that," answered Mr. Larson with a laugh. "Come this way, and I'll *show* you what we're talking about. The Submarine Canyon is one of the wonders of California. Follow me!"

How the Sea Otters Made History

Just then there was a commotion behind them. Turning to look, Johnny saw that people from all around were hurrying to the windows of a huge tank. On the next floor up, Johnny could see more people on a balcony looking into the tank and laughing and pointing.

"What's going on?" he asked Jody.

"They must be feeding the otters!" Jody exclaimed. "Can we go watch, Mr. Larson?"

"Oh, you don't want to miss that," Mr. Larson replied. "We'll save the Submarine Canyon for later."

"Come on, Johnny." Grabbing Johnny by the arm, Jody led him to the otter exhibit.

It seemed to Johnny as if everyone in the aquarium had gathered to watch the sea otters being fed. Slipping away from Jody, he worked his way through the people up to one of the windows of the exhibit. Soon he found himself laughing out loud as the furry otters darted about and climbed all over each other, chasing the shellfish and crabs the curator was tossing at them from the side of their pool.

21

After taking a bit of food in their paws, the otters rolled onto their backs and floated happily in the water, using their stomachs for tables. Sometimes the curator held the food in her hand and waited for one of the otters to slide up out of the water and snatch it from her.

"Wouldn't it be fun to have her job?" asked Jody, who had managed to squeeze through to the front of the crowd.

Johnny shrugged. "I guess so," he said carelessly.

"Oh, Johnny," Jody teased. "You just don't want to admit that this isn't so boring after all."

Johnny made a face but said nothing. The feeding time was over, and the crowd began to drift away. "Come on," sighed Jody, "Vito and Mr. Larson are waiting for us."

"Well, did you enjoy the show?" Mr. Larson inquired when the four of them were together again. "That's one of the most popular attractions here at the aquarium."

"At the aquarium, maybe," frowned Vito, "but those little devils sure wouldn't win any popularity contests among fishermen."

"The fishermen don't like them?" questioned Johnny. "How come?"

"Well, no one can deny they're cute, and smart too," Vito replied. "A little *too* smart. You see, they beat the fishermen to a lot of abalone and other shellfish."

"I don't care how mad the fishermen get!" exclaimed Jody. "I think otters are California's most important animal. Someone should build a statue in honor of them."

"What for?" challenged Johnny. "Just because they're cute and eat lots of crabalone—or whatever you call those things—doesn't mean they deserve a statue."

"It's not because of those things, smart-aleck," Jody replied hotly. "It just so happens that the otters had a lot to do with how California got to be settled. Isn't that right, Mr. Larson?"

"You remember your lessons well, Jody," answered Mr. Larson with a smile. "Without the sea otter, the whole

history of California would have been different."

Vito shook his head. "The whole history of fishing, maybe," he muttered, "but otherwise I agree with Johnny. I can just see you trying to convince the boys in the fishing fleet that the otter should have a statue!"

Mr. Larson grinned. "It looks like you have a couple of skeptics, Jody. Why don't you tell them the story of the sea otter and see if it doesn't change their minds."

"Yes, do tell the story," said a woman's voice. Looking around, Jody was surprised to see that a group of women had stopped to listen in on their discussion. Suddenly she felt very embarrassed.

"Go ahead, Jody," Mr. Larson urged. "I'll help you out if you get stuck."

"We'd all like to hear it," said the woman who had spoken before. Jody saw that she had a yellow badge pinned to her blue overcoat. The other ladies all wore yellow badges too—some kind of club, Jody thought.

Looking at the people waiting expectantly, Jody felt her heart pounding. Oh, why did I have to start an argument? she thought. Glancing at Vito, she saw him give a little nod and a wink. "We're all ears," he said gently.

"Yeah, all ears," echoed Johnny sarcastically.

All right, thought Jody. Being annoyed with Johnny somehow made her feel braver. *All right.* She cleared her throat nervously.

"Well, a long time ago," she began, "on the other side of the ocean, there were people who thought the otter skin was really special. In fact, in China the otter skin was the royal fur! Because the skins were so hard to get, people were willing to pay a lot of money for them. Then, in 17... uh..."

"Seventeen forty-one."

"Thanks, Mr. Larson. In 1741 a ship got stuck on a freezing cold island way up in the north, somewhere around Russia or Alaska. A man by the name of Vito—

whoops!" She giggled nervously. "I mean a man by the name of *Vitus* was the ship captain."

"Vitus was his first name, Jody. Can you remember his last?"

Jody hesitated. "I can't remember, Mr. Larson," she confessed. "All I know is that a bunch of things up there were named after him."

"That must have been Vitus Bering," commented Vito.

"Yes, that's it," Jody agreed. "And it was the Bering Sea."

"And the Bering Strait," said the woman in the blue overcoat. She smiled encouragingly. "Please go on."

"Right, the Bering Sea and the Bering Strait," Jody continued. "In fact, I think the island his ship was stuck on is even called Bering Island."

"What's all this got to do with putting up a statue for sea otters?" questioned Johnny.

Jody scowled. "I'm getting to that, Johnny," she whispered. "Just be patient." Raising her voice, she resumed her story. "After the shipwreck, the Russian sailors had to build a smaller boat from what was left of the one that was ruined. That took a lot of time, and a lot of work. Of course, it was super cold, and there was hardly anything to eat. Some of the sailors died before the work was finished—including Vitus Bering himself!"

"What about the otters?" insisted Johnny, but this time Jody ignored him.

"Trying to keep from starving," she went on, "the sailors killed and ate whatever they could find. They even ate some sea otters!"

"No! Really?" exclaimed the woman in the overcoat. Even Johnny looked a little shocked at the thought of eating otters.

Jody nodded. "I don't suppose they liked the otter meat very much, but it helped keep them alive. Just as important were the otter skins. The sailors made warm coats and rugs and things like that out of them. So it was the otter skins that helped to keep them from freezing until

the boat was finished and they could go home."

"And that's why the otters should have a statue?" asked Johnny. "Because they saved a bunch of Russian sailors?"

"No, Johnny, that's just the beginning. You see, when the sailors went home, they were wearing their otter skins. They probably didn't even know how valuable they were. Well, since everyone thought the men had been lost at sea, it was big news when they got home safely. And that's how people heard about the otter skins."

"Remember, Johnny," Mr. Larson chimed in, "otter skins were precious. Now a lot of people knew where they could be found—in some of the relatively unexplored areas of the North Pacific. That knowledge prompted fortune hunters to organize expeditions, and with that, the great otter hunt began."

As Mr. Larson was talking, Jody glanced around and saw that her audience was growing as passers-by stopped to join the small crowd of listeners. She felt a shiver run down her spine. She was teaching all these grownups about California history! Taking a deep breath, she picked up where Mr. Larson had left off.

"The great otter hunt was sure a good name for it. From the islands in the North Pacific, the Russians worked their way down the coast of Alaska, and then Canada, and finally all the way to California, looking for more and more otters. And that brought them into country that the Spanish wanted for themselves.

"Well, when the Spanish heard about these Russian hunters, they began to get pretty nervous. Somehow they had to let the Russians know that the Spanish were claiming that land. The trouble was, they really hadn't settled this part of California yet."

"I see," Vito said thoughtfully. "You mean that the Spanish moved north because the Russians were coming down the coast. And it was all because of those furry friends of yours."

"Right!" Jody replied. "And so the Spanish settled

Monterey, and that's why California became Spanish instead of Russian."

"Boy, I bet the otters were glad when the Spanish showed up," observed Johnny loudly. He wasn't about to let Jody get all the attention.

"I don't know about that," Mr. Larson put in. "Unfortunately for the otters, things didn't get much better for them after the Spanish arrived. So many people continued to hunt them for their fur that eventually they almost died out. For many years people thought they were gone for good."

"You mean like the sardines?" Johnny asked. "Then how come there's some in the tank?"

"I said they *almost* died out," Mr. Larson reminded him. "But a small group of them managed to survive along the cliffs down by Big Sur. During the 1930s some of them were spotted playing in the water."

"And that's how people found out that they weren't extinct after all," Jody concluded.

"Hmph," grunted Vito. "I've got to admit I had no idea otters were such important characters or that they came so close to disappearing."

Mr. Larson nodded. "Not many people do, Captain. When people do realize how few sea otters are left, they begin to understand why they are protected by state and federal laws."

"And why they should have a statue," Jody added.

"I couldn't agree more, young lady," said the woman in the overcoat. She stepped out from the crowd. "Let me introduce myself. I'm Josie Jacks, the director of Monterey's Golden Age Club, and my friends here are all members." She waved a hand at the circle of women around her. They all were beaming at Jody. "On behalf of all of the Golden Agers, I want to thank you for such an interesting talk. Why, I had no idea the otter was such an important little fellow! If a statue fund ever does get

started, be sure to give us a call. I think we'd like to be part of the fund raising campaign."

"We surely would," said another of the Golden Agers. As the other women murmured their approval, Josie Jacks reached into her purse.

"Oh, I can't take any money now," Jody whispered.

Josie laughed. "I'm not looking for money," she replied. "Ah, here we are." She took out her hand and held up a shining yellow badge. "Young lady," she announced, "I would like to make you an honorary member of the Golden Agers." She leaned toward Jody. "You're not quite old enough, you know," she added in a low voice, "but you are wiser than your years." Smiling broadly, she pinned the badge on Jody's raincoat and gave her a friendly hug. All at once the hall was filled with the sound of the women clapping. Vito and Mr. Larson joined in, too, and so did the rest of the crowd.

"Well done, Jody," Mr Larson applauded.

"Bravo!" beamed Vito.

Jody felt herself blushing. "Thank you," she murmured politely, looking at the floor. After what seemed a long time, the clapping died away, and the crowd broke up into groups of twos and threes.

"Come along, ladies," said Josie Jacks to her friends. "There are lots more fascinating things to see yet! Goodbye, young lady!" Waving and smiling, she and the other Golden Agers moved off down the hall.

Bashful

"Wow!" laughed Jody when the people had gone. "I wonder if that's what it's like to be famous." Proudly she touched her badge.

"I suppose now you want your own statue," Johnny grumbled.

"Actually, I feel like hiding in a hole," Jody confessed. "I never gave a speech before."

Vito glanced at his watch. "Speaking of hiding," he said, "it's about time I showed you that creature I promised you. Hiding in holes is one of the things he does best."

"You mean the one that shoots around like a jet plane?" asked Johnny.

"Well, I didn't exactly say he shoots around like a jet plane," Vito laughed. "But let's go find Bashful and you can see for yourself."

"Bashful!" echoed Johnny as they followed Vito down Marine Mammal Hall. "Why do you call it that?"

"You'll see," Vito replied mysteriously. "By the way, there are some pretty interesting critters in there, too." He pointed to a huge tank they were passing. Inside were hundreds of fish of all sizes and shapes.

"Wow!" exclaimed Johnny, craning his neck. "This tank is taller than my house!"

"It's about three stories high," Mr. Larson explained. "It's the tallest aquarium exhibit in the country. By the way, all those fish you see can be found right here in Monterey Bay."

"Including the sharks," Jody added with a shiver.

"What are those little silvery fish swimming in a big bunch?" Johnny asked. "They look like they're playing follow the leader."

"Those are sardines, Johnny," answered Mr. Larson. "When they're in a group like that we call it a school."

"Ugh!" Johnny grunted. "Did you have to mention school?"

"Sorry," replied Mr. Larson with a laugh. "By the way, sardines have a certain fame around here too. You see . . . "

"I know," Johnny interrupted. "They're the fish that made Cannery Row famous. Right, Vito?"

Vito grinned. "Right you are, Johnny. Only in my day people were more interested in eating them than in looking at them."

"Seems like you know a few things yourself, Johnny," Mr. Larson remarked. "Can you tell me anything about those big plants?"

Johnny peered into the exhibit. Tall, skinny plants rose high above his head and swayed gently in the water. Looking up at their tops, he felt as if he were walking under water. "Are they seaweed?" he asked.

"Very good! They're a special kind of seaweed called giant kelp. As you can see, they grow thick and tall. In fact, this exhibit is known as the Kelp Forest. It does feel like you're in an underwater forest, doesn't it?"

"Sure does," Johnny nodded. "Or else a jungle."

"How did the kelp get to be so tall, Mr. Larson?" inquired

Jody. "Does it grow especially fast?"

"It does, indeed, Jody. In fact, along certain sections of the California coast, it's said to be one of the fastest growing plants in the world. If the conditions are just right, it can grow up to twelve inches a day."

Jody whistled. "A foot a day! I'll bet your friend Bashful can't do that, Vito!"

"Well, he may not be able to grow a foot a day," Vito acknowledged with a chuckle, "but he does grow eight arms."

Johnny and Jody looked at each other. "An octopus!" they cried at once.

"Right you are, mates," Vito replied. "And he's right over here." Waving his hand for his friends to follow, Vito rounded a corner and headed for a darkened chamber. "Take a look in there," he said, pointing to a tank window.

Stepping to the window, Jody and Johnny gulped in amazement.

"Now that's awesome," breathed Jody as they both stared, wide-eyed. The creature Vito called Bashful was spread across the window of the tank, its eight snake-like arms stretching in all directions.

"How can he stick to the window like that?" Johnny asked at last.

"He's got those things like suction cups under his arms," answered Jody. "See? He's using them to walk."

As they watched, Bashful moved slowly across the window. In a moment Johnny found himself looking straight in the eye of the octopus. "Hey, if that's Bashful, he's sure not living up to his name!"

Almost as if he had heard Johnny's remark, the octopus suddenly took its tentacles from the window and shot to the opposite end of the exhibit. A brownish cloud spread through the water where he had been.

"Did you see that?" exclaimed Johnny. "I see what you mean about a jet engine, Vito! But what's that brown stuff?"

"And how did it move so fast?" Jody wondered. "And why did it go backwards?"

"One question at a time, please," laughed Mr. Larson. "As you saw, the octopus usually gets around by using its arms, which are called tentacles. But if it has to, it can move a short distance in a hurry by drawing water into its body through its gills, and then shooting it out through a funnel. The funnel is like an exhaust jet on a rocket. By forcing the water out, the octopus gives itself a push."

"Like a jet engine," Vito observed.

"Right. As for moving backwards, the octopus is more streamlined that way, so it can move faster. And that cloud is a kind of ink it releases to confuse its enemies while it gets away."

"Pretty neat," Johnny said, looking back into the tank. "But where'd he go? He's disappeared!"

"Look closer, Johnny," Mr. Larson suggested. "Bashful does like his privacy, so he's trying to trick you into thinking he's gone."

Peering into the window, Jody and Johnny studied the opposite end of the exhibit looking for hiding places. "All I see is rocks," muttered Johnny. "Wait a second! Did that rock just move?"

"That's him!" Jody cried. "He changed color so that he looks just like the rocks now. How'd he do that?"

"That's one of the things that makes the octopus so magical," Mr. Larson replied. "Not only can it change color to match its surroundings, but its skin can become either smooth or rough, just like the rocks, or sand, or whatever it is hiding in."

"Wish I could disappear like that!" laughed Johnny. "Especially when it's time to do the dishes."

Jody giggled. "But just think how fast you could do them if you had eight arms! Oh, but speaking of arms, can an octopus really grow a new arm if it loses one?"

"It sure can," nodded Mr. Larson, "although it won't be quite as large as the original. But that's not all of the story.

The octopus has a number of other interesting features, too. Its eyes are highly developed, more like a human's than a sea creature's. It has three hearts instead of one, and when it bleeds, its blood is blue! Best of all, it can ooze through tiny openings much smaller than its body. In fact, the only hard part of its body is its mouth—really a beak, like a parrot's. If it can get its beak through a hole, or a crack in the rock, then the rest of it can squeeze through, like toothpaste."

"Look, he's doing it now!" Jody exclaimed. They all looked just in time to see Bashful's head squeezing through a crack in the rock no more than an inch wide. Soon the last of his arms slithered into the crack. The octopus had disappeared!

"Squish!" marvelled Johnny.

Mr. Larson shook his head wonderingly. "Well, well, I guess we'll have to plug up that hole when he comes out. I thought we got them all."

"Will he come out?" worried Jody.

"Oh, yes, he'll come out for food. Which reminds me—"

"That it's time to eat," finished Johnny. "I'm starving."

"Well, no," laughed Mr. Larson. "I was going to say that reminds me of a story. But if you're hungry, why don't we head on down to the cafeteria for a snack? I'll tell you the story while you eat."

"Good idea," agreed Vito. "These old legs can't take too many more stories without resting a bit. Come along, mates, my treat!"

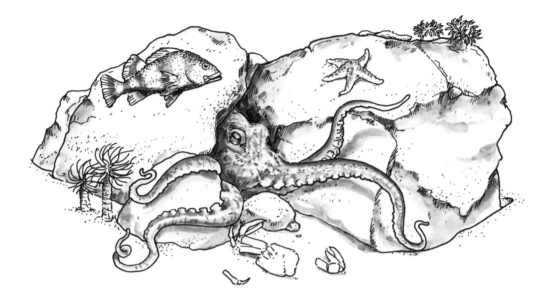

The Case of the Missing Crabs

The aquarium's cafeteria was a bright room with large windows overlooking the bay. Vito treated Jody and Johnny to sodas and hamburgers, and all three joined Mr. Larson at a table by the window.

"That octopus sure is a special creature," Jody remarked when they were all settled.

"Yeah, 'specially ugly," mumbled Johnny through a bite of hamburger.

"That's not nice," scolded Jody. "If you were his father, you wouldn't think he was ugly."

"If I were his father, I wouldn't think at all," Johnny retorted. "Because I wouldn't have a brain."

"I'm afraid you're wrong there," Mr. Larson broke in. "Actually, the octopus has a sizable brain. As a matter of fact, the intelligence of the octopus has a lot to do with the story I was going to tell you. You might call it 'The Case of the Missing Crabs.'"

"Could you please tell us now?" pleaded Jody.

"I thought you'd never ask," smiled Mr. Larson. "I should

explain that I heard this story from my brother, Fred, who is a marine biologist at another California aquarium."

"He's a what?" interrupted Johnny.

"A marine biologist. That's a scientist who studies life in the sea. As you can see, that's an interest that runs in the family. I suppose we get it from our father's experience working with Captain Bruno here."

Vito nodded approvingly. "Of course I was mostly interested in *catching* life in the sea," he said. "But I must say that the older I get, the more fascinating it is to learn about all there is in that watery world." Something in Vito's tone made Johnny look at the old man. Vito was staring out the window at the waters of the bay. Looking at the pale scar on his nose, Johnny wondered again where it had come from. More than ever, he was sure that Vito knew more tales of the deep than he was telling—and he could bet that one of them would explain the scar.

"Well, to go on with the story," Mr. Larson resumed, "Fred had just started working at the aquarium when he made an interesting discovery. It seems that there was a tank of crabs kept in a private area, not far from an octopus tank. What Fred discovered was that some of the crabs were disappearing! They weren't dying or anything like that— they simply vanished, a few at a time.

"Naturally, Fred decided to keep a closer watch on the tank. After many checks, he realized that the crabs must be disappearing at night, after everyone went home. And that just made the whole thing even more baffling. Finally my brother decided he would just have to spend the night at the aquarium and see if he could solve the mystery.

"So, one night Fred brought in a sleeping bag and bedded down right in the room where the crab tank was— and the octopus tank too, you'll remember. In the dead of night, he was awakened by a scraping noise. Switching on a flashlight, he saw that the lid on the octopus tank had been pushed up. No one was in the room. Fred was just about to get up and investigate when out came the

octopus! It hauled itself right out of its own tank, down the side, and across the floor to the tank that held the crabs."

Jody's mouth fell open. "The octopus opened its own tank?"

"Yep," nodded Mr. Larson. "I told you it was smart! Then, when it reached the crab tank, it climbed up and over the side and disappeared. In a moment it was coming out again, holding a nice tasty crab in one of its tentacles. Making its way back to its own tank, the octopus climbed in, crab and all. Wasting no time, it closed the lid and returned to its favorite crevice to enjoy its midnight snack.

"As you can imagine, Fred was amazed at what had taken place, though he was relieved to solve the mystery of the missing crabs. Just to be sure, the next morning he cleaned out the octopus tank to see what he might find. Sure enough, hidden in a narrow crevice were the remains of several crabs."

"Wow," said Jody. "Pretty neat, huh, Johnny?"

Johnny wrinkled his nose. "Aw, I don't know about that story. Are you sure your brother didn't make it up, Mr. Larson?"

"Johnny!" Jody exclaimed. "That isn't nice at all. Of course Mr. Larson's brother didn't make it up."

Mr. Larson raised a hand. "Johnny's right to question what he hears, Jody. In fact, at first I found the story hard to believe myself. But since then I've done some research on my own. It turns out that octopuses in other aquariums have also been known to leave their tanks in search of food—and make their way home again. Octopuses have even learned how to unscrew the lids of jars to get at a treat inside."

Vito shook his head. "I knew those eight-armed creatures could grow to quite a size, but I had no idea they were so smart."

"How big do they get?" wondered Johnny.

"Nobody knows for sure, Johnny," Mr. Larson replied thoughtfully. "Over the years there have been some pretty

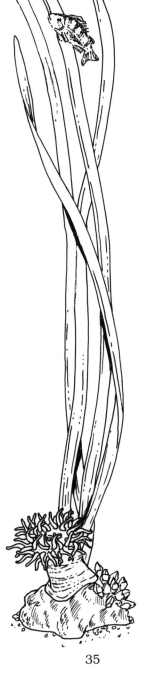

fantastic claims. According to one story, the remains of tentacles from a huge octopus were found in the stomach of a whale. After a lot of oohing and aahing, someone did some measuring and figuring, and the result was amazing. From the tip of one tentacle to the tip of another, the octopus that whale had eaten for dinner would have measured more than one hundred feet!"

It was Vito's turn to be doubtful. "In other words," he said slowly, "you're talking about an octopus that was as long from end to end as a great blue whale!"

"That's exactly right, Captain—if the story is true. But, as they say, 'you ain't heard nothing yet'! An even stranger tale goes back almost a hundred years. In 1896, the partly decayed remains of a mysterious sea beast washed ashore on a Florida beach. People from all over came to see it and to guess what it might be. Finally, a marine biologist said that the remains were part of a giant octopus—a really giant octopus! In fact, this creature was so huge that hardly anyone could believe it was an octopus—including other scientists. In the end, the marine biologist decided that perhaps he had been a bit hasty in his decision. He then announced that the remains were probably those of a decayed whale.

"That seemed to please the people along the Florida coast. They felt better knowing there were no multi-armed monsters lurking off their shores!"

"If the creature was just a whale, why are you telling us about it?" Johnny interrupted.

"Hold on, Johnny," Mr. Larson replied. "If you'll give me a chance to finish the story, you'll see what I'm leading up to."

"I'm sorry," Johnny apologized. "It's just that you were talking about octopuses, and then you got all wrapped up in a rotten old whale."

"Thank goodness I wasn't really wrapped up in that smelly beast!" Mr. Larson laughed. "But let me get back to my story. After the marine biologist said that the creature

could have been a whale, things calmed down, and the remains were soon forgotten.

"And they stayed forgotten for almost seventy-five years. Then that stubborn beast turned up again! It seems that a portion of the remains had been preserved in alcohol. Somehow they wound up at the Smithsonian Institution in Washington, D.C. In 1970, a slice of the creature was studied with advanced scientific techniques."

"And it turned out to be an octopus after all!" Johnny guessed.

"That's right, Johnny. To everyone's amazement the beast's tissue structure was that of an octopus." Mr. Larson turned to Vito.

"Now, here's the incredible part, Captain. If these findings were accurate, that octopus's tentacles would have had a span of about two hundred feet."

"Two hundred feet!" Vito exploded. "Why, that's longer than half a football field!"

"Wow," Johnny breathed. He tried to picture an octopus stretched out over most of a football field.

"I agree that it's hard to believe," Mr. Larson admitted, "but the story has been written about in more than one publication."

"Gosh," exclaimed Jody with a shudder. "I've read stories about giant squids and things wrapping their arms around sailing ships, but I always thought people made them up. Could they be true?"

"I don't know, Jody," Mr. Larson replied, "but that Florida beast does make you wonder."

Vito rubbed his beard thoughtfully. "You know, sailors used to call octopuses 'devilfish.' Maybe that was a good name for them."

"Did you ever see a giant octopus attack a boat, Vito?" Jody asked.

"No, no," laughed Vito. Then his face grew serious. "No, not an octopus," he added softly, glancing at the water outside the window.

"Aw, I bet people just made up all those stories," said Johnny. "There's no such thing as 'monsters of the deep.'"

Vito swung around to face Johnny. "What makes you so sure, son?" he said sharply. The old man's eyes glowed fiercely.

"Now, now," Mr. Larson interrupted. "It's right to be skeptical about tales of wonders—at least until you have proof. Besides, the creatures we do know about are strange and wonderful all by themselves. And a lot of them come right into California's coastal waters." He pointed out the window. "In fact, if you kids are done eating, why don't we have a good look at the Monterey Bay Habitats Exhibit? And then I'll show you what I promised you before—the Submarine Canyon, one of California's true wonders."

"I'm done," Jody announced as she slurped the last of her soda.

"Me too," said Johnny.

"Coming, Captain?" Mr. Larson asked as he stood up from the table.

Vito shook his head. "These old sea legs aren't what they used to be. I think I'll just continue to sit for a spell and catch up to you a bit later."

"You'd better be careful," laughed Jody. "Bashful might sneak out of his tank and get you!"

"Oh, I'll watch out for Bashful," Vito answered with a smile. "You just be sure Johnny sees all there is to see. And speaking of good-sized creatures, don't forget to look for the sunfish. There are a couple of new ones in the exhibit, and they're a handsome size."

"We'll do that," Mr. Larson promised. "Come along, kids."

At the door to the cafeteria, Johnny stopped to look back at Vito. The old fisherman sat quietly at the table, gazing out the window at the waters of the bay. He seemed to be lost in thought.

Johnny felt a tug at his sleeve. "Come on, Johnny, Mr. Larson's waiting for us." With a last glance at Vito, Johnny followed Jody out of the cafeteria.

The Mysterious Submarine Canyon

Catching up to Mr. Larson, Jody and Johnny strolled with him to the Monterey Bay Habitats Exhibit. As they approached the immense tank, Johnny stopped to look in a bubble window. "Hey, Jody," he called. "Look in here. It feels like you're in the water." Suddenly his eyes grew wide. "Look at that!" he gasped.

Peering into the window, Jody and Mr. Larson saw that Johnny was nose to nose with a fierce-looking shark.

"Oh, don't worry about him," Mr. Larson laughed as the shark swerved away. "He's only a sevengill shark. He probably wouldn't pay much attention to you if you were in there swimming alongside him."

"No thank you!" Johnny exclaimed. "You can go swimming with him if you want. I think I'd rather just watch from here."

As they walked alongside the exhibit, Mr. Larson told Jody and Johnny about the different kinds of fish and other creatures they were seeing. There were wolf-eels, spiney dogfish, giant sea bass, bat rays, starfish, and many others. "If you'd like to feel a bat ray or pet a starfish, there are special displays where you can do that," he explained. "By the way, what do you suppose those two sizable creatures are?" He pointed to a spot near the top of the tank.

"Well, they're big, and they're round," Johnny replied. "They must be the sunfish Vito was talking about."

"Very good! Now for the grand prize, can you tell me why they're called sunfish?"

"Because they're big like the sun, and round like the sun," Johnny answered confidently.

Jody shook her head. "Sorry, young man. You don't win the aquarium after all," she teased.

"Okay, show-off, why are they called sunfish, then?" challenged Johnny.

"Don't be mad, Johnny. I said the same thing you did the first time I saw a sunfish," Jody answered. "But the guide told me it was because they like to swim near the surface, where the water is warmed by the sun."

"That's right, Jody," Mr. Larson agreed. "Incidentally, those guys might look big, but I've seen pictures of one sunfish that weighed around three thousand pounds! Believe me, he would make our specimens look like midgets. Can you guess where that giant was caught?"

"Out in the ocean?" Johnny ventured.

"Nope! Right here in Monterey Bay."

"See, Johnny?" Jody said proudly. "Monterey Bay is pretty special."

"Special enough to make the *Guinness Book of World Records*," added Mr. Larson. "And more than once, too. Some years back, the Guinness book told about a twenty-foot octopus that was trapped in a fisherman's net right here in the bay. And another creature that was caught in the bay was a real world beater—a huge Pacific leatherback turtle. Ever seen one of those, Johnny?"

Johnny shook his head. "I don't think so."

"Well, this kind of turtle is pretty impressive. Normally it

40

grows to about six or seven feet in length and weighs around seven or eight hundred pounds."

Jody whistled. "Whoa! I had a pet turtle once, but it wasn't even as big as my hand!"

"What about the Monterey turtle?" asked Johnny. "How big was it?"

"That's the interesting part," Mr. Larson replied. "It was more than twice as heavy as the usual leatherback. In fact, it weighed nearly two thousand pounds! Not only did that guy come right out of Monterey Bay, but it also made the *Guinness Book of World Records* as the largest known creature of its kind in the world."

"Hurray for Monterey Bay!" Jody exclaimed. "The *Guinness Book of World Records*—isn't that something, Johnny?"

Johnny frowned thoughtfully. "But how come Monterey Bay has all these big creatures?" he asked. "Is it really different from other places?"

"I think it is, Johnny," Mr. Larson answered. "Come this way, and I'll show you why."

Johnny and Jody followed Mr. Larson into a darkened hallway. On the wall was a large map of Monterey Bay. As Johnny watched, different parts of the map and wall panels lit up to present information about the bay and its shoreline.

"If you look right here," said Mr. Larson, pointing to the map, "you'll see what may help to explain why so many rare and large creatures have been spotted in Monterey Bay. This area is the great Submarine Canyon—an enormous underwater trench. It's so big, in fact, that the Grand Canyon in Arizona would fit inside it, with room to spare! Those deep, dark waters are only beginning to be explored. Who knows what rare and strange creatures might be dwelling there?"

"Aye, who knows?" said a familiar voice. "More rare and strange than you might think!"

"Vito!" Jody exclaimed as she spun around. "Where did you come from?"

"Oh, I just washed in with the last wave," Vito replied with a wink. "But go on, Bill, I want to hear what you have to say about rare and strange creatures."

"Me, too," said Johnny.

Mr. Larson laughed. "What's the matter, Johnny? Aren't giant turtles and octopuses enough for you?"

"And three-thousand-pound sunfish," Jody added. "And great blue whales." She showed her teeth. "And sharks!"

Vito rubbed his nose. "Aye, and wolf-eels and bat rays, and flatfish. And how about sheephead? They start out as girls and turn into boys! But I think there are stranger things even than those."

"Spoken like a true fisherman, Captain," said Mr. Larson with a chuckle. "But one very strange creature that does come to mind is the ribbon fish. There was one caught nearby that wound up at the Smithsonian Institution."

"Just like the Florida octopus," Jody remembered.

"That's right, Jody. However, in this case the people at the Smithsonian were able to study the whole fish and not just some partial remains."

"Why is it called a ribbon fish?" Jody asked. "Because it's long and skinny?"

"That's exactly right," Mr. Larson replied. "I understand some people also call it an oarfish. Whatever you call it, it's an odd-looking beast, and relatively rare. In fact, some people think that the ribbon fish or oarfish may be the explanation for sightings of supposed sea serpents."

"Are they that big?" questioned Johnny. "Could they really look like some kind of sea monster?"

"Well," said Mr. Larson, "there are accounts of oarfish-like creatures that have washed ashore that were in the neighborhood of fifty feet long. That's longer than ten Johnnys laid end to end."

"Sounds a bit like the Loch Ness monster," Vito observed.

"That it does," Mr. Larson agreed. "Interestingly enough, Loch Ness is in Scotland, and one sighting of a huge oarfish happened in the Orkney Islands, which belong to Scotland. But as we've been saying, you don't have to leave California to find mysterious creatures."

"Mysterious enough!" muttered Vito.

"Besides being long and skinny, are oarfish strange in any other way?" Jody asked.

"Oh, yes, they're different for a number of reasons," Mr. Larson replied. "One special thing about them is their ability to get away from an enemy minus a good part of their body."

"Ugh! How does that happen?"

"It may be one of its defenses, Jody. When a shark, or some other creature, bites off a part of the oarfish's body, the rest of it manages to escape while its enemy busily eats the portion it has bitten off."

"That's weird!" Johnny exclaimed. "What else makes them different?"

"Good grief! How many reasons do you want?" laughed Mr. Larson. "How about the fact that they are able to swim near the surface of the sea with their heads sticking out of the water? Does that make them different enough for you?"

"You really mean it? No wonder people thought they were sea serpents."

"That's not all, Johnny," Mr. Larson continued. "The oarfish also has what appears to be a reddish crest, or mane, on its head and along its back. In the words of a marine biologist, this would probably be described as a modified dorsal fin. Apparently, when the creature becomes alarmed, the dorsal fin stiffens and stands up. People who have seen this rather odd-looking fin have said it looked like red hair."

"A red-headed sea serpent!" Jody giggled. "That *is* weird."

"Well, I'll be," muttered Vito, rubbing his nose. "I wonder if that explains it."

"Explains what, Captain?"

"Why, Bobo, of course! The Old Man of Monterey Bay!"

"Bobo!" Johnny laughed. "That sounds like a clown."

Vito glowered at Johnny. "I assure you, Bobo was no clown!" the old man snapped.

Startled, Johnny took a step backwards and glanced questioningly at Jody. What had he said to make the old fisherman angry?

"Maybe I should explain what the Captain is referring to," said Mr. Larson hastily. "You see, stories of Bobo have been around for years. Bobo was supposed to be a beast of some kind that was spotted from time to time in Monterey Bay. It was called the Old Man of Monterey Bay because, well, some people said its face looked like a man's."

"And he had red hair!" Vito added earnestly. "Or—or so they say."

"Gee, why didn't you tell us about him before?" asked Johnny. "Bobo sounds like the strangest creature of all."

"You wouldn't have believed me if I had," Vito replied. "You're the type that needs proof. Don't get me wrong, Johnny, that's a good quality to have. The only problem is, Bobo is not the kind of creature you're going to find in a book on fishes."

"Besides, there's no proof the creature really exists," cautioned Mr. Larson. "Isn't that right, Captain?"

"No—no proof," Vito mumbled. "Just what some old fishermen say, that's all."

"Tell us," pleaded Jody.

"Yeah, tell us," echoed Johnny.

Vito shook his head. "As Bill says, there's no proof. It's just that that oarfish creature sounds a bit like descriptions I've heard of Bobo, that's all."

"Tell us about the descriptions, then," Jody said excitedly. "Was Bobo big? Did he look like a serpent? Did he ever come close to shore?"

"Excuse me for interrupting, Jody," Mr. Larson broke in.

"But it's nearly four o'clock, and I've got to take a turn at the information booth. I'll leave Bobo to Captain Bruno here. I'm sure he knows more about him than I do. Enjoy the rest of your stay, and be sure to say goodbye before you leave."

With a wave of his hand, Mr. Larson headed for the information booth.

"Thanks, Mr. Larson," Jody called after him. "Now, Vito, please tell us about Bobo."

The old man gave a deep sigh. "Well—all right. I guess I shouldn't have mentioned him if I didn't want to talk about him. But if I'm going to tell you the tale, we may as well get comfortable. Let's go see if we can find a seat on the patio. When I left the cafeteria, I saw that the sun was peeking out, and our coats will keep our bottoms dry even if the benches are a bit wet."

The Old Man of Monterey Bay

Eagerly, Johnny and Jody followed Vito to an outdoor patio overlooking the aquarium's huge tidepool. From the patio they could look out on the waters of Monterey Bay, the home of the many wonderful creatures they had seen in the aquarium's displays. Above them, the clouds were breaking up, and patches of blue sky were starting to appear.

"That's quite an interesting place," Vito remarked, pointing to the tidepool. "A little world of creatures all its own. You'll have to learn all about it next time you come. Meanwhile, let's have a seat on this bench over here, and I'll tell you the strange tale of Bobo, the Old Man of Monterey Bay."

As they took their seats on the bench, Vito breathed in deeply. "Ah, smell that salt air! Isn't it grand? And listen to those sea lions barking! I'll tell you, mates, you can roam far and wide through this great world, but there's no place like home."

"I'll say!" Jody agreed. "Monterey's pretty neat after all,

isn't it, Johnny?"

"Sacramento's neat, too," Johnny retorted. "It's the state capital, you know. And it never rains there. We get sunshine every day."

Vito chuckled. "Well, that sounds like just a bit of an exaggeration, son, but you're right. Sacramento is a fine place, too. In fact, this whole state of California is grand, full of beautiful country and all the history and adventure anyone could want." The old man nodded thoughtfully. "Yes, and mystery, too—like Bobo!"

"Tell us about him," Jody begged, hugging her knees to her chin. "Do you think he was an oarfish? And how did he get such a funny name?"

"Ah, there's a tale in that," Vito replied. "It has something to do with that comment you made, Johnny, about Bobo sounding like a clown."

"Honest, Vito, I wasn't making fun of him," Johnny apologized. "I've just never heard of a sea serpent with a name like Bobo."

"I know, lad." Vito smiled. "You see, it's just that many people do have a tendency to make fun of Bobo—and of the people who say they've seen him. In fact, that may be how Bobo got his name."

"What does teasing people have to do with his being called Bobo?" Jody asked.

"Well, perhaps I'd better start at the beginning," Vito answered. "And then it will all make sense. Listen carefully, now."

"We are!" Johnny assured him.

"All right, then. The story begins back in the 1920s and 30s, when the Row was teaming with canneries, and the sardine was king. As I've told you, there were more than a hundred sardine boats in those days. During the season, they were going out most every day and coming home full of fish.

"Of course, the fishermen brought back more than fish!

They brought back stories, too, of their adventures on the water and in rough weather, and sometimes of the strange creatures they had seen." Vito chuckled. "As you know, fishermen are great storytellers! The biggest and strangest creatures always seem to be the ones that got away."

"Sounds like my dad," Johnny commented. "He likes to fish in the Sacramento River, and he's always talking about the big ones he *almost* caught."

"A true fisherman," Vito observed with a grin. "Anyhow, over the years, more and more stories began to be told of a strange sea beast in the deep waters of the bay. Too many stories, if you ask me, to be pure invention.

"Then, one day back in the 1920s, a young fisherman— only a teenager, actually—frantically rowed his one-man boat to the Monterey wharf. He had been fishing a long way from shore, and by the time he reached the wharf, he was exhausted. After he tied up his boat, he climbed slowly up the ladder to the main level of the wharf. Every step seemed to be an effort. Some other fishermen were standing about, and they could see that the young man was pale and shaking. 'What's wrong?' they asked him. At first, he shut his mouth tight and refused to say. But as they continued to pepper him with questions, he finally sat down on the wharf and told his story.

"It seems the young man had been scared half out of his wits by the strangest sea creature he'd ever seen. It was long, like a serpent, yet it had the head of a man! The creature had looked the young man right in the eye, so he said, and he swore that the eyes were almost human!"

"Ugh," shuddered Jody. "No wonder he was scared."

"Well," Vito continued, "the young fisherman had wasted no time once he saw the creature. He'd grabbed his oars and rowed home as hard and fast as he could, and never looked back.

"Now, when he tried to tell his story to the other fishermen, how they laughed at him! They teased him without mercy, and told him to 'quit acting like a bobo!'"

"Quit acting like a bobo? What did they mean by that?" asked Johnny.

"Patience, my friend! It seems that these were Portuguese fishermen that the frightened young man was talking to. According to my Portuguese friends, the word 'bobo' means something like a fool or a dunce. So, when someone says 'Quit acting like a bobo,' it can mean quit acting silly—"

"Or quit acting like a clown!" Johnny interrupted.

"Exactly. You see, you were right, Johnny. 'Bobo' does mean something like 'clown.' And for years after this sighting, many other fishermen who saw strange creatures in Monterey Bay were afraid to talk about them for fear of being teased and called a bobo. In time, the name stuck to the creature itself—the one the young fisherman said he had seen, which also came to be known as the Old Man of Monterey Bay."

"Did other people see it, too?" asked Jody.

"Oh, yes. Over the years, the creature was seen so many times that eventually it became a favorite topic of conversation along the waterfront. A lot of folk said it was all a tall tale, but I can't agree. Too many people saw it over a period of too many years. There was something out there, all right. Maybe there still is."

"But what exactly did they see?" asked Johnny. "Did they really see a man's face?"

"What about its body?" Jody chimed in. "Was it long and thin, like a sea serpent? Did it have arms like an octopus?"

"I guess I'd have to say it was more serpent-like than anything else," Vito replied. "But you must remember that there are almost as many descriptions as there are people who say they've seen the creature. Some of the fishermen I've talked to say that Bobo was as long as a telephone pole, but much wider. Still, about all they ever saw of it was its head and neck, and maybe a hump or two along its back."

"What about its head? Was it shaped like a man's?" Johnny asked.

"Could be," Vito nodded. "Again, the descriptions differ.

But a number of witnesses described the head as being strangely human-like. I remember many occasions when fishermen gathered on the wharf and talked in hushed tones about how much the beast reminded them of a person—especially the mournful look on its face, and its evil-looking eyes."

Vito paused and shut his own eyes for a moment as a slight shudder seemed to race through his body. "Matter of fact," he continued with an embarrassed grin, "I sometimes get the shivers myself when I think about those eyes!"

"Ugh!" Jody said again.

"Aw, I don't know about these stories," said Johnny. "Maybe people imagined the whole thing."

"A whole boatload of people?" Vito shot back.

"What do you mean?" Jody asked.

"Just what I said! It wasn't always a single fisherman who saw Bobo. There was one time when a big sardine boat drifted right up to the creature, and several men got a look at it."

"What was it like? Did anyone get a picture?"

"No, no pictures, Jody. That always seems to be the way it is with mysterious beasts of the deep. No one seems to have a camera."

"That figures," said Johnny. "No proof."

"No proof," Vito agreed. "But this story is hard to disbelieve. It was even written up in the local newspaper when it happened, back in the late 1930s. I saved that article, and I've read it many times. There's hardly been a word about Bobo since then. No one has seen him, as far as I know, for many years now."

"What did the article say?" questioned Jody excitedly.

"Well, as I recall, the headline was 'Old Man of Bay Back on Top—Weird Monster Sighted Again.'"

"Monster!" Jody exclaimed. "Did they really see a monster?"

"Let me finish," replied Vito. "Then you can decide for yourself. It seems that a sardine boat was passing over the Monterey trench—the Submarine Canyon—when one of the crew spotted what appeared to be a huge white face in the water.

"He shouted for his shipmates to look, and in a matter of moments the entire crew was staring at the creature. The face was described as four feet wide." Vito spread his arms. "Even wider than this!"

"Wow," breathed Jody.

"The creature seemed to be asleep," Vito resumed. "Then, as the boat drifted to within a few feet, the beast awoke with a snort and flashed coal-black eyes at the crew.

"Apparently, the creature was startled by the nearness of the boat and the sight of the gawking fishermen. It snorted again, dug its fins into the water, rolled over, and dived out of sight. Except for the face, most of the crew got only a glimpse of the monster—or whatever it was—before it was gone.

"Later on, when the fishermen returned to Monterey, news of the sighting spread throughout the waterfront. Soon the incident was being reported in newspapers up and down the coast.

"The most amazing part of the story was how the fisherman who first spotted the beast described its face. He said it looked like the face of a monkey—or of a very old man." Vito chuckled. "I'm not sure I like that comparison!"

"You don't look anything like a monkey," Jody assured him.

Vito patted her hand. "Thank you," he said with a smile. "But there was more. The creature's eyes were said to be twice the size of breakfast buns, and its mouth was shaped like a crescent moon. There were barnacles all over its head, and folds of white skin hung beneath its neck.

"As for its body, the creature was described as being around thirty feet long, about as big around as a pick-up

truck, with a fish-like tail. The fisherman guessed that the beast must have weighed eight or nine tons. That's about eighteen thousand pounds—quite a heavyweight, if you ask me."

Jody giggled. "Sounds like Bobo needed to go on a diet."

"Maybe he did," Johnny commented sarcastically. "And he lost so much weight, he wasted away to nothing. That's why nobody can see him anymore."

Vito shook his head in dismay. "That's exactly why I don't like to talk about Bobo these days. Most people just make a joke out of it."

"Don't say that, Vito," Jody begged. "If you believe in Bobo, then that's good enough for me—well, maybe. Anyway, it's no joke, that's for sure."

Johnny frowned and shook his head. "I'd like to believe in him, too. But I'd believe in him more if I saw him for myself."

Vito gave Johnny a friendly pat on the shoulder. "I understand, Johnny. If I were you, I'd probably feel the same way. But I'm an old man who has fished in the waters of Monterey Bay most of my life. I've learned to hear such tales with more of an open mind. After all, I've experienced some strange things in these waters myself! And you must remember that I've only told you about two of the Bobo sightings. Believe me, if we had more time, I could tell you Bobo stories for the rest of the afternoon."

"That's just it," Johnny said disappointedly. He cupped his chin in his hand. "Those are stories you've heard from other people. It would be a lot more exciting if you'd seen Bobo yourself."

"That *would* be exciting," Jody agreed with a sigh. "But that was a good story anyway, Vito. Thanks for telling it."

Vito's Secret

Vito was silent for a long moment. Suddenly he stood up. "I think I should let you in on a little secret," he announced. "It's a secret I've kept for many years."

"About Bobo?" Johnny exclaimed.

Instead of answering, Vito began to walk briskly across the patio. "Come this way," he commanded. Scrambling to their feet, Johnny and Jody followed him to the far end of the patio, where it jutted out over the water. At the railing, Vito stopped and pointed across the bay.

"See those smokestacks?" he asked. "They mark the site of the community of Moss Landing. Right in that area is a big slough."

Johnny wrinkled his nose. "What's a sloo?"

"It's like a small inlet of the bay, Johnny, a marshy place where water stands. This one is called—"

"I know," Jody interrupted. "It's called Elkhorn Slough. My dad says it's somewhere around there that the Submarine Canyon starts."

"That's right, Jody. Elkhorn Slough is known for many

53

other things, too, especially for the variety of birds that gather there." Vito smiled grimly. "I know it best for another reason. I was headed out that way, you see, when Bobo gave me this souvenir!" The old man raised his hand and pointed to the scar on his nose.

"Bobo gave you that?" blurted Jody.

"You really saw him?" cried Johnny.

Vito nodded. "I really saw him, Johnny. At least, I saw something very strange! I've been collecting Bobo stories ever since, trying to find the explanation for what I did see—and proof that I saw it!

"You see, Johnny, that young fisherman I told you about—the one everybody laughed at and called a bobo— that was me. I don't know whether that's really how Bobo got his name, but I do know it's no fun to be called a clown. I learned to keep my mouth shut, after that."

Johnny blushed. "I'm sorry," he mumbled, looking at the ground. "I didn't know you were talking about yourself."

"Of course you didn't," Vito said gently. "I purposely left out the part about the gash on the young fisherman's nose, or you would have guessed for sure. I didn't want to mislead you, but I've kept my secret for many years now, and I thought I'd go on keeping it. Besides, I still don't relish being thought of as a bobo." The old fisherman laid a hand on Johnny's shoulder. "You know something, young man? You were right to doubt the story. In your place I would do exactly the same."

"What did you see, Vito?" asked Jody. "Was it like you told us—a serpent with a man's face?"

"To tell you the truth, Jody, I can't be sure after all these years just what I saw. What happened was this. I had just taken my bearings by sighting on the entrance of Elkhorn Slough when I saw a big log sticking out of the water. I was trying to row my boat around it when I got the shock of my life. All on its own, what I thought was a log turned in the water and faced the boat."

54

Jody shivered. "What did it look like? Was it Bobo?"

"I'd never heard of Bobo in those days," Vito answered. "All I know is, this creature had a head like a man's. At least, that was my impression. What I mostly saw was its eyes—and its red hair."

"Red hair!" echoed Johnny.

Vito nodded. "It had reddish hair on its head that hung straight down. That's as much as I can be sure of. In a flash the creature was under water—and I was rowing for shore as fast as I could go. More than the hair, it was those eyes that scared the daylights out of me—those terrible eyes."

"So that's why you were interested in the oarfish!" Jody cried. "Because of the red mane Mr. Larson was talking about."

"That's right, Jody. After all these years, I'm still seeking the explanation for what happened to me so long ago. There are times when I wonder whether I didn't dream the whole thing."

"But what about the scar?" Johnny demanded. "You said Bobo gave you that—and that's real for sure."

To Johnny's surprise, Vito laughed out loud. "Ah, yes, the scar. You're right, Johnny, it certainly is real. And Bobo did give it to me—in a way."

"But how?" Johnny frowned. "You said he just disappeared under the water. Did you see him again another time?"

"No, Johnny, I never did—though I looked often enough! There was never a night or day on the water, in all those years of fishing, that I didn't keep an eye out for another glimpse of the Old Man of Monterey Bay. But I never did see him again."

"Then how—?"

Vito chuckled. "I'm afraid it's not a very heroic story, Johnny. You see, when I saw that strange face and red hair in the water, I simply panicked. I reached so hard and fast for the oars that I smacked myself in the face with one of the grips. I opened a pretty good gash, too. And that's how I got my scar. I'm afraid that all it proves is that a young man was very frightened and very careless. Exactly what frightened him, no one can ever say for sure."

"Wow," said Jody, shaking her head. "That's some story. I wish Mr. Larson could hear it."

"Did I hear my name?" someone called.

"Mr. Larson!" Turning around, Jody saw her former teacher hurrying toward them.

"The very same," smiled Mr. Larson. "I've been looking all over for you. There are a couple of anxious ladies at the entrance who are very interested in the whereabouts of a certain young man and lady at—let's see—four-twenty and counting."

"Oh-oh," Jody groaned. "We got so caught up in Vito's story that I forgot all about the time. We'd better run, Johnny! Oh, Vito, thank you for—" Jody stopped short as she looked at Vito. The old man was touching a finger to his lips. Jody understood. His secret would be safe with her.

"For telling us all those old fishermen's stories," she finished.

"Yes, thank you, Vito," added Johnny with a knowing smile.

Vito gave a little bow. "The pleasure was mine, mates. And Johnny, if you visit again, you be sure to come say hello to an old friend, you hear?" He held out his hand.

"I will!" Johnny promised, trying not to wince as the strong hand of the old fisherman closed on his own.

"Yes, do come again, Johnny," Mr. Larson added. "It's always nice to share the aquarium with people who are really interested. You probably won't believe this, but I tried to get one of *my* fourth-graders to visit, and he wouldn't come. Do you know why? He said he thought the aquarium would be boring!"

"Huh!" Johnny snorted as Jody tried not to giggle. "I

know what I'd say to *him.*"

"Oh you do, eh?" said Vito, giving Jody a wink. "And what would you say?"

"I'd say, quit acting like a bobo!"

Mr. Larson looked quizzically at Jody and Vito. "What does he mean by that?" he asked them. "And what's so funny?"

But they were too busy laughing to answer.

Author's Notes

Otters, Octopuses and Odd Creatures of the Deep is the second book in the History and Happenings of California series. As with *Stagecoach Santa,* the first book in the series, the story is fiction, but it includes many facts—some of them rather startling! These Author's Notes provide further information so that readers can better appreciate the incidents described in the story.

The **Monterey Bay Aquarium** is located at the north end of Monterey's famed **Cannery Row.** As Vito tells Johnny, Cannery Row gained its name from a novel by the great American writer **John Steinbeck.** A Nobel laureate and Pulitzer Prize winner, Steinbeck knew the Row well during the days when Monterey was the Sardine Capital of the World.

In the late 1800s, though, the most prominent feature near the site of the future aquarium was **Chinatown,** a quaint fishing village featuring crooked streets and houses built on stilts over the bay. For many years, the skills and customs of the Chinese fishermen and their families made the Monterey Peninsula a more colorful place. Oriental-style fishing boats plied the waters of the bay, illuminated at night by red pine fires (hung basket-like over the sides) to attract squid. Tragically, Chinatown burned to the ground in 1906, never to be rebuilt.

Ten years later, in 1916, the Hovden Cannery opened. One of the first canneries on the Row, the Hovden Cannery was the last to close, ending its days in 1973. Little did anyone know that in 1984 the cannery's location would become the site of Cannery Row's latest claim to fame—the Monterey Bay Aquarium.

During the construction of the aquarium, care was taken to preserve the exterior appearance of the old cannery. Inside, however, the building was just as carefully being designed to house one of the largest and most dramatic aquariums in the nation.

With over 5,000 living specimens and more than eighty displays, the Monterey Bay Aquarium is a "must" for visitors to California's beautiful Monterey Peninsula.

In backing up these words of praise, let me briefly elaborate on two of the displays mentioned in the text. The **Monterey Bay Habitats Exhibit** admired by Jody and Johnny is ninety feet long. It contains about 326,000 gallons of water and more than 1,500 living creatures. In addition to the **sunfish** and **sevengill shark** discussed in the text, the exhibit also contains striped bass, copper rockfish, strawberry and white-plumed anemones, bat stars, sablefish, king salmon, sanddabs, starry rockfish, steelhead, big skates, leopard sharks, giant acorn barnacles, and many other interesting creatures. One of the display's most dramatic features is a pair of bubble windows that allow visitors to get a "fish-eye" view of underwater life.

The **Kelp Forest Exhibit,** as Mr. Larson explains, is three stories high. Housed within this immense facility are many types of sea creatures, including rubberlip surfperch, sheephead, Pacific sardine, horn shark, turkish towel seaweed, decorator crabs, giant green anemones, and red abalone. The exhibit's star attractions, though, are the **giant kelp plants.** These remarkable brown seaweeds are among the fastest growing plants in the world.

Other incidents mentioned in the text that refer to the wonderful characteristics of California's marine life are well documented. **Sea otters,** of course, are among the best-loved residents of the coast. Their rediscovery in the 1930s was front-page news and a cause of much rejoicing. Less well known is their significant role in California history, as related by Jody and Mr. Larson. Who knows? Perhaps one day there will be a statue erected in their honor, to remind us of their unique place in our history.

As for the two Monterey Bay creatures that made the *Guinness Book of World Records,* references to both the

Pacific octopus and the giant **Pacific leatherback turtle** can be found in the 1975 edition. More recent editions tell about the giant octopus that washed ashore on a Florida beach in 1896. The story about the octopus that was in the habit of selecting crabs from a neighboring tank for its evening snack was shared with me by a number of knowledgeable people. A similar account of an eight-armed "thief" in England can be found in the Reader's Digest book *Marvels and Mysteries of Our Animal World.*

Certainly one of the marine world's marvels is the **ribbon fish,** or **oarfish.** The specimen described by Mr. Larson was caught in Monterey Bay in 1938. A beautifully prepared cast of the creature was presented to the Santa Cruz Museum by the Smithsonian Institution in Washington, D.C. It is on display at the Santa Cruz City Museum, 1305 East Cliff Drive, Santa Cruz, California.

All the creatures described so far are only a fraction of the rich and varied life that can be found in and around Monterey Bay. Many marine biologists believe that the bay's great **Submarine Canyon** plays an important role in bringing unusual and fascinating creatures into the bay. This immense canyon is only beginning to be explored, and many more forms of underwater life may be discovered there in the future.

Just one example of the mysterious types of marine life already found in the Submarine Canyon is an almost magical creature known as the *Colobonema.* A type of jellyfish, the *Colobonema* was described by a noted researcher as "the most beautiful animal in the ocean." (The researcher caught a specimen—on videotape—in the Monterey Canyon in 1985.) Among the more colorful characteristics of this creature is its ability to send an electric blue light pulsing through its tentacles, apparently to distract its enemies. On occasion, the *Colobonema* puts on an even more dramatic show in the darkened depths of the sea by shedding its tentacles in a burst of light. This is also done for defense purposes and may be a "last gasp" way for the *Colobonema* to escape the jaws of a hungry fish.

Who knows what other marvels await us in the shadowy depths of the Monterey Canyon? With odd creatures like the *Colobonema* dwelling in those dark waters, could there also be something even stranger—such as the creature Vito knows as **Bobo, the Old Man of Monterey Bay?**

At this point I should explain that although Captain Vito Bruno is a product of my imagination, I modeled him after some very real people. In fact, much of the Bobo information that appears in this book came from an aged Montereyan who was the main inspiration for my fictional character. This respected fisherman was at the wheel of a sardine boat in 1934 when he spotted a red-headed sea beast that resembled, in part, the famous Old Man of Monterey Bay. Much of the other Bobo information, including the tale of how the mysterious beast may have gained its name, was told to me by other old-timers of the Monterey waterfront.

These California fishermen are proud people who delight in discussing their exploits and the part they played in helping Monterey to become the Sardine Capital of the World. Some of these old-timers also remember their encounters with Bobo, and they willingly discuss their experiences with those who share an interest in odd creatures of the deep.

After tracking a number of these people down, and listening to their tales, I must admit I have gained an even greater respect for them. There are those who believe that Monterey Bay's mysterious sea beast was nothing more than a member of the elephant seal or sea elephant family, but I can't help but think there is more to the story. An especially convincing witness is a former purse-seiner captain who first saw the creature in the 1920s. This man had seen elephant seals and the like many times. What he saw on that long ago day, he said emphatically, certainly did not resemble a member of the sea elephant family!

One of the best-documented accounts of Bobo is the newspaper story described by Vito. The story appeared in the October 21, 1938 issue of the *Monterey Peninsula Herald,* and its contents are faithfully reflected in Vito's retelling.

But perhaps Mr. Larson is right after all. Whatever may explain the Bobo sightings, there are plenty of strange and wonderful creatures in California's coastal waters to go around. You could spend a lifetime learning about otters, octopuses, and odd creatures of the deep. As Johnny and Jody discovered, a good place to start is with California's own Monterey Bay Aquarium. If you get the chance to visit, I know you won't find it boring!

In concluding these Author's Notes, I would like to thank the many people who provided information or verified facts used in this book. I am especially grateful to Dr. Steven Webster, well-known marine biologist and director of the Education Department at the Monterey Bay Aquarium, and to the other members of the aquarium staff. In addition, I would like to thank several educators and librarians who graciously took the time to read the story in manuscript form and offer helpful comments. They include Cynthia Bergez, fourth-grade teacher, Stuart Hall for Boys, San Francisco; Donna Bessant, district librarian, Monterey Peninsula Unified School District; Margaret Ceresa, coordinator, library services, Evergreen Elementary School District, San Jose; Rhoda Kruse, formerly senior librarian, California Room, San Diego Public Library; Kay Niemeyer, coordinator, school library services, San Diego County Office of Education; Barbara Schubert, English/language arts coordinator for Santa Clara County and past president of the Santa Clara County Reading Council; and Judy Wilcher, fourth-grade teacher, Berryessa School District, San Jose.

Finally, my sincere thanks to the many old-time Monterey fishermen who shared with me their tales of long ago.

About the Author

Randall A. Reinstedt was born and raised on California's beautiful and historic Monterey Peninsula. After traveling widely throughout the world, he spent fifteen years teaching elementary school students, with special emphasis on California and local history. Today he continues to share his love of California's beauty and lore with young and old alike through his immensely popular publications. Among his many books is **More than Memories: History and Happenings of the Monterey Peninsula,** an acclaimed history text for fourth-graders that is used in schools throughout the Monterey area.

Randy lives with his wife, Debbie, and son, Erick, in a house overlooking the Pacific Ocean. In addition to his writing projects, he is in great demand as a lecturer on regional history to school and adult groups, and he frequently gives workshops for teachers on making history come alive in the classroom.

About the Illustrator

David F. Aguero was born and raised in the Monterey Bay area. Since attending the Academy of Art college in San Francisco, he has worked for several years in the fields of illustration and design.

David is a commercial illustrator with a broad range of interests and talents. He is especially known for his airbrush and pen-and-ink illustrations.

Randall A. Reinstedt's
History and Happenings of California Series

Through colorful tales drawn from the rich store of
California lore, this series introduces young readers to the
historical heritage of California and the West. "Author's
Notes" at the end of each volume provide information about
the people, places, and events encountered in the text.
Whether read for enjoyment or for learning, the books in
this series bring the drama and adventure of yesterday to
the young people of today.

Currently available:
Stagecoach Santa
ISBN 0-933818-20-3

Otters, Octopuses, and Odd Creatures of the Deep
ISBN 0-933818-21-1

*California history and lore are also featured in Randy Reinstedt's
books for adults and older children. For information about these titles,
please write Ghost Town Publications, P.O. Drawer 5998, Carmel,
California 93921.*